A Poet Praying for Peace

Ahmad 'Da Silencer' Durant-Bey

BookLeaf Publishing

India | USA | UK

I dedicate this body of work to

Horace Durant-Bey,

Goldie Roberson,

Maurice Smalls,

Ahmir Durant-Bey,

Jamir Durant-Bey,

and to every poet of the past, present, and future.

~Rest in Poetry Lorna Pinckney~

Acknowledgments

I would like to thank the curators of Divine Tectonics, Etymology, Fuzzy Wednesday's, Verses, Busboys and Poets, and Spit Dat where I was able to learn and develop my craft. Special thanks to Raquel Brown, Droopy the Brokeballer, Queen Sheba, and Lorna Pinckney. Thank you to the men of Omega Psi Phi Fraternity Inc., especially Fall '05 Pi Gamma. I would also like to thank Lot 14, Ashley Bush, Tierra Veney, and Ronald Harris III who have supported me from the start. Behold!

Preface

Like most writers, my journey began with a burning curiosity. I wondered if I could ever have such an impact and connection with my words as some of my favorite writers. This practice allowed me to witness my growth over the years. My brother took me to my first open mic at Mango's in Washington DC, when I was 17 years old. I remember wearing dress clothes to blend in with a mature crowd. After witnessing an array of talent, which to me seemed like handpicked premier stars, I decided I would do this for the rest of my life. A few weeks later I got a tattoo of a hand holding a microphone over my heart with the words "Till Death Do Us Part." I developed my skills as a writer while attending Norfolk State University. My peers welcomed my words with open hearts. Their reception encouraged me to explore my creativity deeper, becoming more and more vulnerable in my writing.

This book of poems was sparked by the goal to document 10,000 hours of writing as I came across a 21-day writing challenge. At the time I was reading Natalie Goldberg's "Writing Down the Bones," which was a guide to getting first thoughts on paper. I was able to pull myself away from my usual perfectionist approach of trying to figure everything out all at once. I began to do timed sessions with one goal in mind, to keep my hand moving the entire time. I found a new level of freedom pursuing consistency in my craft while silencing my inner critic. I could have gone through a rigorous editing process, made each line rhyme, and presented stanzas pruned to please the eye. Instead, I embraced my imperfections in hopes for you to get a glimpse of my thoughts as they developed organically. Now I have the privilege of sharing my experience with you.

Put pen to paper and let the writing reveal itself.

Revival

Whatever you're growing through
Grace looks good on you
Remember you need space for your roots to
release
You need room to breathe
Dedicated chambers to remind yourself of
yourself
There's a life to be lived outside of paying bills
Build it with the intention to stand the test of
time
Your militancy needs nurturing to balance the
scales
There is a designated speech set aside for self
Don't go days without checking in
If there's too much going on in your world for
a moment of peace
Soon will come a time you won't be in the
world
Now, what's really important?
The demands you feel obligated to won't wake
the dead
I pray poetry does

Missed the Bus

Perhaps your plans fail because you don't plan
properly
Did you plan to be on time instead of early?
Well, then you planned to be late
Improper planning says your goals can wait
So when things don't go your way
Be prepared to be tutored by time in the art
of patience
Some things you can control
So what's your investment in your own
success
I hope you're not waiting for opportunity to
come to you
Like your dreams are supposed to be on
DoorDash
That's asking to be on someone else's time
Too often we say what we want
But where is the sense of urgency?
The sirens should sound before the state of
emergency
Have you ever watched a piece of paper

Wear the spark of a flame then be consumed
by the fire?
That's what your transmutation takes
Don't be afraid of changing forms
If your font is failing to get the point across
Become the flame and be glad to be ash
It could be that you are the fuel to light the
way
Why submit to fear and not show up whole?
There's no satisfaction in only presenting
what you perceive as perfect
Perfection is the entire cycle of growth
And you've been known to skip stages
Look at the moon in all of its phases
See your beauty from all angles like the
diamond you are
Dive deep into the darkness and the unknown
Love all your imperfections on this path
That's what makes a good day great
Praise potential,
But raise the bar with your walk
And show up ahead of time

Recalibrating Questions
Pt. 1

Who am I?
What am I doing?
Where am I going?
Questions recalibrating soul with purpose
I often have to evaluate
My state of consciousness
Just so I can determine
Who's driving and who's passenger
Sometimes at night I wrestle
With the aftereffects of amnesia
My compass starts computing
And I realize I've drifted off course
Head to the sky, I study stars
Gathering clues about my coordinates
Did I fall asleep at the wheel?
Or has my ship been seized by pirates?
Not sure what happened during the blackout
All I know is I'm back now
Pushing things I can't change to the
background
Placing my present state under a microscope
My 3rd eye needs a final observation
Maybe there was a stage for wandering
A lesson plan teaching me to go with the flow
Now the rhythm of my intentional breath

Sets my sail
I have a mission to complete
That I must see through
This part of the course requires
My full attention
And I intend to take responsibility
For my own success

Cleanup Hitter

I've walked through war zones
Posted up on the same corners where worlds
collide
Sworn secrecy for sheisty faces seeking
atrocities
I'm not tongue tied, Tightlips, I'm only
telling the truth
Family broke bread leaving my home
abandoned
Would you believe neighbors welcomed me
with open arms
Closed palms clothed colt handles in my
defense
I don't need security, but I get why you would
The temperature rises and minds flip switches
A caged bird can sing a song in an instance
There are no receipts to buy back innocence
On summer nights try not to cry over spilled
milk
Man, my childhood can fill the well in the eye
of Horus
Guess that's why I was appointed the role of
eternal scribe
Some sins are never forgotten like fallen
soldiers

I share stories in the attempt to build a level
of sanity
Living with skeletons for so long
Bedrooms became tombs
Been writing psalms in songs before I knew
who was author
Fully aware of my power to pull swords in
rocky situations
Mountaintop missions propel preferences
perfecting penmanship
More of a man still content with this pen pal
in my hand
The unfulfilled promises of people never
returned my letters
Shipwrecked in a bottle is the only time I
manage to break open
My birthday wish is a way to better navigate
depression
Facing north with a smile, so they won't see
me in another mask
There's gotta be a life worth living in this
story somewhere
Retracing my steps for clues to where I left
my wallet

I don't wanna go to Mexico no more, more,
more
Take me home I'm tired of sleeping on park
benches
Since I made this bed
There's comfort in changing the sheets
I can start over
Now it's time for spring cleaning
Let the oldies play

Everyday Truths

Today is the first day of the rest of your life
Each task determining the outcome
No decision is more important than this one
In this moment you have the ability to set a
standard
Execution is a kin to success
Sign the contract and stay committed
This isn't about one day, one week, or one
year
It's about the consistency of precisely placing
a brick
This is the groundwork
Now breathe and be present
Set the foundation for future generations to
flourish
It's not about how to spend a fortune
It's about sowing seeds of gratitude
That will one day lead to trees in a forest
you'll never see
This life isn't about you, but what you will do
with it
Exercise your gifts and make your mind
flexible

Your awareness is the rudder determining
your course
Don't be tossed by storms and forget your
destination
You have everything you need to be great
Why settle for a good life when you were
meant for more
Make room for the blessings you prayed for
The doors will be open and you will break
bread with strangers
Wash the feet of lost souls and spark a
resurrection
All it takes is for you to remember your
worth
Stick to the plan and watch the plan produce
fruit
Trust in the season
For the soil needs the rain
Sun will come in due time and raise your
vibration
Your frequency will make the blind see the
light
Live like you know how priceless your steps
are in this world
Ordered by a higher power

Silver and gold can't compare
Faith is measured in your response to
opposition
I hope you know the universe conspires in
your favor
Have peace

Rhythm to Events

Fall leaves crawling across the street
Gracefully forfeiting their vibrancy
The sun shines
Playing peekaboo with the world
As the clouds dance before our eyes in swirls

There's a rhythm to events, no coincidence
Pieces land where they're destined
On either side of the fence
Acceptance is a superpower
You must channel your strength
Developing picture-perfect patience
In moments of suspense

In tune I'm separated from emotions that are
fleeting
No longer chasing relationships that aren't
worth keeping
So much energy expended on things that
don't matter
We must really reevaluate what it is that we're
after

Math multiplies as days pass and seconds
become hours
Showing up is half the battle
In presence there's power
My range expands when I take my hands and
lend them to God
The way is revealed and the path doesn't seem
as hard

My desire is to be the best version of myself
when I serve
Remaining steadfast avoiding the crash when
life throws a curve
I smile in the face of opposition now that I
see the light
Even failure works in my favor when I know
I'm living right

No justification for juxtaposition
Just a jump or leap of faith
I'm living in my purpose
Even through storms I can't escape
Forward march to victory
Can't be distracted by the noise

Remember who you are
And whose you are to remain poised

Just keep working it will work itself out
Just keep working it will work itself out

Connecting Trains

I let my pen walk and my wins talk
I only converse with the Universe
There's a priceless reverence for presence
Unity is no longer a concept, but a way of life
The road beneath my feet grounds me
With no anchor holding me down I am free
to roam the clouds
Sipping from teas and streams as light beams
Dancing across bodies of water in the corner
of my eye
My pen possesses the caress of a lover's touch
Take my time as I undress my thoughts upon
these sheets
We make music that the masses stream
My aura is an overheard conversation
manufacturing smiles
Imagine the songs trees sing to me when I
meditate in the wild
I can hear the longings now loud and clear
Her bark wants to know me like man's best
friend
My only relationship is with the All
I am all I need and this awareness inspires
hope

I've witnessed wells overflow simply because I
was close
What greater deeds will He do for me in my
time of need?
Success is no longer steps I take, but every
breath I breathe
Yahweh. Victoriously! Use me as U see fit
Condition my way of thinking to be in
alignment
Let the world see the majesty of this crown
I am a hope reviver, a dream investor
A leader of elevated thinking
The time has long called for a new train
conductor
Connecting communities
And He's right on time

Blessed to Give

Gifted
Wrap me in paper
Put a bow on my back
Remind yourself of the goodness of giving
Set your intentions
Think about the smile that will emerge
When this gift is presented
The feeling sweeping over you is a gift in itself
Best thing about this model is it never goes
out of style
Take pride in knowing you struck gold
This ain't about materialism
It's about feeding the soul
I promise you
This is the gift that keeps on giving
Waters from my well will wash over you
Blessing generations to come
Place this time around in a frame
Dedicate me to your mantlepiece
As a living testimony to peace of mind
Day after day, embark on this treasure hunt
Eyes wide like Yolanda's heart for what you
may find
I'm trying to tell you

This is one for the ages
History will praise you for your contribution
For there are some blessings you can't keep to
yourself
Some things are meant to be shared with no
hesitation
This present will reignite communication
during fellowship
This is communion
It's been awhile since you knew in your heart
of hearts you were the church
We've been long overdue for a testimony
Let the world know in group text there's
something they need to see
Let old friends be mesmerized when they
discover
The gift was little ol' me
Finally my family tree can see the light of
divine nature
Stretch branches to the sky in praise
I a man, I a sinner, I am redeemed
I take back my power and align all faculties
Place my pupils on the Most High
The teacher becomes the understudy of my
playpen

Point to a corner of the Earth and watch my
light shine
Somebody needs a reason to be thankful
I'm grateful it's me
Hand deliver me to the hearts of the hopeless
Tell them help is on the way
I am a gift I can't keep to myself
It would make my heart too heavy if I tried
I give my all to thee
Just wait till you see what's inside

Elementary Meditation

The very first time I meditated was in
elementary
I'm not sure what prompted the practice
One day I decided to spend the day in silence
A one-child protest in the middle of class
I remember hearing with such clarity
The interruption of intercoms screeching
Chalk stuttering producing dotted lines
Lockers closing conversations and jokes
I smiled tuned into my teacher's instructions
Being present without participating felt
natural
As I observed the world around me
I gradually noticed my internal dialogue
My stillness moved peers without me moving
a muscle
Their attentiveness diverted from the lesson
of the day
More concerned with the stance they noticed
me taking
This awareness became contagious and swept
the room

Imagine having so much attention while
seeking self
After awhile, friends started to check on me
Like "Are you ok? I mean you're here, but
you're not here, here."
It wasn't like me to hold my tongue back then
Too much shotgun personality to take the
backseat
The longer I refrained
The more concerned they seemed
They began to speculate about what could've
happened
Dancing around landing on the idea of me
being invisible
The expectation of playing my role never
crossed my mind
Then someone said the fatal words
"Maybe he's just sad because his dad died"
(dad died, dad died, dad died)
The reverb struck a nerve
Making me smile off key
I could no longer keep my composure
Nor could I contain my emotions from the
thought

Tears flooded my face trying to escape my
reality
I just wanted one day
One day to not be seen
Not knowing it was too much to ask
The precedence had been set unbeknownst to
me
But for a moment I found peace
Meditating in elementary

The U and Me

It's never too much to bear
Until they see the polar opposite
Not until the strings of sanity pop
Then suddenly humanity is possible
The stronger you prove to be
The more weight they try and pile on
Like if I endure the final stretch
Then they'll just move the pylon
To be uncomfortable is one thing
To be purposely inconvenienced is another
Some lessons are taught by father time
Being taken for granted is a mother
Nothing worse than wasted energy
That leaves you feeling spent
Then looking up to no one around
Cold shoulders make cold hearts convinced
It's just me and the All
Even though I crave community
It would be nice to have a friend
But sometimes it's just U and me
It's best to become better accepting
Than bitter neglecting the truth

The proof is in the reflection
In the mirror, it's just you
When you came here and when you leave
Will be the same
When judgment calls
Finger pointing won't suffice
There's only one to blame

Liberation lies
In knowing it in your heart
Nothing new
Just the same lesson you've known from the
start
I expect more of me now
Than I do from others in my past
Something clarifying my thoughts
With the reality I cast
Strength has been renewed in turmoil
Turbulence delivered me to peace
I know frequencies I wouldn't notice
In an uneducated space
Grateful for room to grow when I was green
Hopeful for the days to come
Confirmation speaks to me like an inside joke
I dance to a deeper drum

One that can't be drowned out
Because the beat is forever present
I'm tuned in to a different degree
My aum is omnipresent
Can't take this away
There's no need to debate
My name was written far before you could
run
Or walk this way
I give my all to the All
Make of me as U see fit
I was tailor-made to endure
And do more than simply exist

Messages to a Mirror

Grace will never forget your face
The Universe knows you by name
Trees bend to shade your path
Waters are distilled as you watch
The wild gathers in awe of you
Hearts are warmed by the thought of you
A generation is waiting praising all you do
Love is forever present
No thing is impossible
Have faith in the Sun when the Moon is new
Don't neglect details rushing for nothing
Your only goal is getting to know you better
No one else will truly understand if you don't
take the time
Meditate in crowds by removing yourself
from the noise
Dissect the differences between hunger,
cravings, and convenience
Even when the road isn't clear, step out on
faith
Be early when it's time to show up for your
dreams

For they reside in a different zone requiring a
deeper focus
Find a cause that draws on your devotion
Live with your entire being or just stay home
Words are empty without action, so how you
gon' act?
You can tell me anything, but your record
reflects
May your friends be mirrors in the Halls of
Amenti
Respect the power given to you and practice
restraint
Abuse is chaos which lacks the harmony of
law
Build
Create
Innovate
Think
Always give back
Helping hands should never be taken for
granted
Wrap your mind around love on a two-way
street
Don't just be transactional

There's more to life than the world will ever
tell
Treasure is buried here
It's up to you to seek it
Don't keep your heart to yourself
Purge your expectations
And overflow wherever you go

Haiku

1

Knocks on summer's door
Fall on deaf ears, I winter
Tend to my own flame

2

A drunken master
Captain Whip Whitaker till
the whip nearly flipped

3

Release me from the
handles of Hennessy and
unhappy hours

4

Feelings could be hurt
Memories can be painful
Call it scar tissue

5

Maya Angelou
Taught me how love liberates
You are free to leave

Recalibrating Questions
Pt. 2

Frequently I ask myself
"What am I doing?"
Or "Where am I going?"
I need to ask myself
Whose I am more often
I don't need vultures and opportunist
Proclaiming to be friends
I need pillars in my life that allow me
To reinforce my foundation
Images that restore features
I may have forgotten throughout this journey
Moving with purpose is only possible
If at first you are in an awakened state
That's why I ask myself questions
I should know the answers to
Shaking off the fog
People, events, food, and technology
Cause ebbs and flows of what I think I know
Too much of anything is bad for you
Divine thoughts will make my body wait for
water
When the well opens to me
I no longer desire to eat
I want to work, be used, be of service

Fill up on joy, overflow fulfilling my purpose
In this moment, I can feel it flowing
I'm here now
No need to navigate where I'm going
I trust the process and I know He's mine
My home is one with Him
There is no separation, but patience needs to
be tested
More connected with the world solo in the
wilderness
Than when I'm connected to wifi in these
polluted cities
I look to the heavens when I want to see my
reflection
The image I see is perfection
Celebrations are deserving for moments like
this
Bliss, when I embrace these gifts
In public, I share what's private
Penetrating the hearts of all
Praises are overdue
And I dedicate them to you
For being present with me

Spartan Women

Spartan women are a blessing
Spartan women are affirmations
Reinforcements for resurrection
The unveiling of revelations
She teaches me to embrace my edges
While nurturing my tenderness
Praising me genuinely for the sake of praise
Not just for her benefit
Her hugs heal childhood traumas
I long to be home again
She is proof that prayer works
Aligning me with the frequency I'm honing in
She speaks life into me with her energy
Making me more than a man
I'm a cosmic farmer, a fruit bearer
More than just a conqueror of land
She sparks my detox
To invest in future generations
Spartan women hit the reset
Spartan women are confirmations
Signs on the highway of life pointing to self
When the road gets hard
Grateful for her grace
Can't know her without knowing her God

She recalibrates unbalanced chakras
So I can pack light
She raises the bar when I'm drifting left
So I can act right
Reminding me of the image I was created in
She's an inspiration
There's no limitation to my creations
And it's amazing
For too long she's had to be strong
When she sees me she's butter
Something in my walk makes her dance
Whether sister, friend, or lover
The delivery of my poetry
Exposes truth in physical form
It's because of her I can weather
Any spiritual storm
Flowers are forever at your feet
For the seeds you've planted for me
If not for your friendship
I would be stranded at sea
Spartan women taught me
That my purpose is true
It's my destiny to avenge ancestors
In service to you

Youniversal

Tallying thoughts is a trust fall
Never knowing when the arms of the
Universe will extend
Not every page is meant to be broadcasted
But in my practice, I've found I'm never let
down
Sometimes it is only in my recap that I realize
The grace that has been bestowed upon my
being
It seems all light can't be seen in real time
The process is there to digest for a reason
Summoning circles back to square one
Back to a clean slate
My imagination still dangles on jungle gyms
at recess
There's always a spot on the sidewalk that
remains naked for me
Caution tape can't convey challenges I
overcome with chalk
Memory lane has become my walk of fame
Hot spots are tubs where the hard knocks of
life are treated
All's well that enswell
No matter where I've been

It's all coming back to me
Talk to me in my sleep,
So when I rise I walk with purpose
My seeds need water
Well wishes aren't enough
I'm working to let go of my ego
Making room for my truth
If they must mention me
I hope it's as an honorable guide
Hashtag, abandon the trend and find a
treadmill
Perfect your breathing sparking sober
thoughts surviving inhales
Storms come, this too shall pass
Sun shines, this too shall pass
Build your hopes on things eternal
And your work will last forever
Stare your morality in the eye,
So you can grin when you see the reaper lying
If you can't take your possessions with you
then find a new focus
Know yourself, what makes you tick, and
what makes you happiest
Be prepared to open your heart when
opportunity knocks

Witness the cosmos bend in your favor
When you own these moments
Listen
Keep what resonates
Discard what's designated "File 13"
Hold onto your joy
Wear your smile like your favorite fit
Any emotion that robs you of glory must be
purged properly
Seek living with a dying urgency every day
SEEK LIVING WITH A DYING URGENCY
EVERY DAY!
Someone will see the light because of your
example
There may not be an award show
Maybe not even a thank you
Always remember who your servitude is in
the name of
Plant people, post-its, and pillars in place to
jog your memory
Don't settle for average
Change the narrative, elevate and claim your
excellency
Royalty comes with responsibility,
But you are worthy of her cause

Raise your children to raise vibrations in any
environment
Don't be the product of an atmosphere
You were meant to breathe life into
Misdirection sounds like guidance from
inexperienced teachers who lived in fear
You are powerful, essential, born to be the
change
There's a wealth of knowledge swimming in
your DNA
Dive in the deep end
Don't be afraid
Your instinct will save you
Plan properly, turn the page, and act often
There's no need to wait
When you'll learn along the way
Why study their curriculum before mastering
self?
The only objective is to distract you from
your own mind
The man in the mirror is the threat they fear
the most
Love him out loud in public and not just for
show
Tell the world love overflows from your soul

It's an honor to be present and a wonder to
be you
I wish I wasn't so hesitant, but I'm grateful
for every stutter step
Each stumble led me to standing tall in the
absence of the crowd
You don't have to be me
You are already you
There's nothing and no one like you
Know love for yourself
Show love to yourself
Show the world what's been missing
Before you wake up one day
Missing what it was like to be
Youniversal

Touching Artwork

Please don't touch
Art is to be admired
Placed on pedestal
Out of reach
Behind a rope
In a case
To be preserved
To be sustained
Without blemish or stain
As to make time stand still
To defy the laws
That we live by
Sparking thoughts
Sparking conversations
Sparking joints
And generations
Looking at the canvas of life
In a new light like
Surpass that

Searching for Mona Lisa

I'm in search of Mona Lisa
My masterpiece
My liberty
The body of work that completes
Stand alone stanzas
Magnify man into myth
Become my living legacy
Mona Lisa

Not sure where this scavenger hunt began
Just hope it has a happy ending
Since a child, I've been infatuated
Graduated and woke up on a mission
A love story worth every brushstroke
Depending upon my poetic depiction
Promise to play your part
And I promise the truth in every sentence
She's the music notes I taste
When I sip a glass of wine
The golden time of day

In the forefront of my mind
When I'm sick of the same word
The synonym on the tip of my tongue
The cinnamon blowing over thresholds
Ushering blessings to come

Her curves hold me hostage
Whenever she's touring
I find the keys to freedom
Whenever she's soaring
A spiritual being is the reason
My smile is beaming today
Her song is the circle of 5^{ths}
To my dancing DNA
There's no match to measure
You would need haiku's breadth
I have waited centuries
To be rejoined with her cycle of breath
She speaks life into me
But where could she be?
Does the beauty I seek
Even have eyes for me?

I'm in search of Mona Lisa
My masterpiece
My liberty
The body of work that completes
Stand-alone stanzas
Magnify man into myth
Become my living legacy
Mona Lisa

Multiple Points of Failure

I had a dream that I lost it all
A laptop and three notebooks
Gone in the wind
I'm pretty sure my mind went with it
A van missing sent me spiraling
Throwing tantrums
I think I was on the verge of tears
Trying to digest this pill known as "reality"
I was almost at the stage of acceptance
When I was sucked back into the abyss
This black hole of helplessness
Struggling to wrap my mind around
"What am I going to do?"
Then it was confirmed there would be no
rectifying this situation
The only reassurance was there was no
insurance
A part of me knew no price could appraise
Intellectual property I mined my soul for
I would've been content with just one win

My attention briefly entertained my usual
crutches
To carry me through a time that seemed like
too much to bear
The loss was too great to be distracted by old
habits
For a moment I thought we would go to war
A lieutenant led us to an armory
Pointed and said, "Gear up!"
I was so ready
Then slowly I started to fumble feeling
weightless
Tossed around like gravity took a vacation
Somehow abandoning me in my time of need
Determined, I fought through my
disorientation
Finally ready to exit the door and engage in
battle
Till I realized the weapons were all props
All of them made for video simulation
Imagine my frustration
In disbelief reliving the turn of events
I woke up with the tender heart of a boy
Who had lost his first love
Then my senses returned everything to me

And I remembered
I have all I need to succeed
But how do I get multiple backups?

Praying in Ink

Sometimes it's a struggle
Walking the tightrope between perception
And the absolute truth
Trying to be honest about how I feel
While speaking abundance and walking in
power
Creating consciously with intent
Is a huge responsibility
Role model or not I aspire to raise vibrations
How do I have this human experience
Without listening to the tide of emotion
Tossed to and fro until I submit to depth
I've never been a surface dweller
More of a nose diver of rabbit holes
When you research the unknown
There's no telling what you'll find
Who you'll become on the other side of
enlightenment
If I'm a changed man maybe I can make man
change
Be a catalyst that catapults the consciousness
of the collective
Maybe my insanity is what's missing from the
world's perspective

I used to think, then write
Now I pray in ink
Let my heart speak, see with my soul
Translations aren't always as accurate as the
vision
But I can't do all the work for you
This is just a nudge, a nod, a note
What's your contribution
How are you improving monuments
And filling the gaps between broken statues
And natural truths
The natural law says I'm attracting you
On a quest to call tribe
But you don't know your name
Wouldn't know my face if you saw it in the
mirror
Or an elementary school yearbook
My relatives no longer relate to me
Freedom of choice creates slavery
I'm taking back my time and attention
My wealth increases exponentially overnight
Finally penetrating to sub-thought
I thought I knew, but it was always U
And in this verse
I see the proof

More to do when there's less of me
Empowered by the whole of us
From the depths I see
Light shining from another galaxy
Found my home in darkness
A star is born again

Pause

Today's generation pauses for all the wrong
reasons
Pause before you speak, so there's no need for
retractions
Pause for a moment to gather your thoughts
There's no rewind in real life
You must live with the tone you established
No one created your statements for you
Speak responsibly, think responsibly
There should be no secondhand smoke from
miscalculated jokes
Pause and reconsider who you are playing
with
Because some people just don't play like that
We allow life to get out of hand
But never pause for reflection
There's no reverence for others housing the
light
We take shine for granted
A little piece of flesh can cause enormous
damage
Don't let the casualties pile up at your feet
Pause before you play yourself
You are your own worst enemy

Our meals are no longer miracles
We don't even pause to pray before breaking
bread
Break old habits and watch time stand still
Pause for those who came and were slain
before you
Pause to praise the efforts of ancestors
The memory of those who tried should never
die
Pause the game and get to know your
neighbor
There's a new experience waiting on a
conversation
Pause the horseplay
It's so important to ride for a cause
So many of us have life figured out only to
wake up lost
Don't get swept up in things that don't matter
Pause and manifest the calling in your heart
Pause out of respect and not for fear of being
canceled
Years will fly by if you don't take the reigns
Pause for the living
Pause for their pain

Pause and be at peace when you miss the
party
Pause for a minute and celebrate yourself
We can't always be present in society
Pause and have patience when you're standing
in line
When you're stuck in traffic, pause
Reflect on what you can control
Let go of what you can't
Pause for discernment
For a chance to catch your breath
Pause and breathe deeply
Remembering you are bigger than your
problems
Pause before begging for pardons
Press forward with right thinking
Your actions will speak volumes when the
time is right
Don't give up the fight to be better than your
past
Pause cause if you don't take a timeout it may
cost you
Pause with intention
Pause and pay attention

A Poet Praying for Peace

My 8th birthday
Was one week after my father's funeral
This poem has lingered on my mind
Like the smell of his rotting corpse ever since
My father was murdered in cold blood
Stuffed in the trunk of his car
They say he went out fighting
I pray for peace... stillness
Questions of confusion
Are the cause behind my distant gaze
I want to be present
You know, stop to smell the roses
But my mind is hijacked by the blood on the
seats
Patches of fabric cut out for evidence
And the smell
The smell that stained my innocence
And soaked into my being
The smell of my father's rotting corpse
An odor so loud
I can barely hear myself think
As I wonder why

Why is a widow and her son subjected to such
an experience?
As if his absence isn't enough
We needed the reminder of riding in death's
DeLorean
Trips to school, work, the grocery store
How is this normal?
What is normal now?
A pen, a piece of paper, and a poet
Praying for peace

Love Letters to God

Some say writing is remembering
I say writing is releasing
Traumatic events and misappropriated energy
All's forgiven once I've given myself to the
process
I submit to stanzas to stand up
In order to run this race I need this pen
This is my second wind sailing me into
victory
There's no place for grudges here
I let go once the crime has been outlined on
pages
My sanity depends on this excavation
Placing these teardrops is breathwork
Without notes I could never know nirvana
Probably wouldn't recognize my own face in
the mirror
This is my true reflection
The one I can see with my eyes closed
My love letters to God
He taught me how to write solely to testify
I've put mileage in poetry in order to survive
Never would've made it to this stage of
understanding

Had it not been for this gift
My imagination led me to develop this level
of patience
I get lost in my work leaving breadcrumbs for
the youth
Yes, I too was an orphan in this life
We may have had different paths, but
overcame similar hurdles
Life prepared us to be strong through trying
situations
The world is in need of a savior
You possess the key to set us all free
Ancestors are the building blocks boosting
you to the top
Do your part
Your effort will never go unnoticed by the
dreamer
Innocent eyes will search the skies for you
You will be the true North for seeking seeds
Who's nature will be to crawl through
darkness
Pursuing a breakthrough unbelievers will try
to talk them out of
Shine today for tomorrow will connect the
dots

Nothing is greater than knowing you're the
one and owning it
Rest, but never give up
Instead, get to it
Your city needs you dedicated
To the details of it's blueprint
Only your tale can complete this task
Don't take this moment for granted
You grant wishes
Demand excellence from your cells
A time will come when you will be a guide
Would you have your inner child deserted?
Would you abandon the heart of the future
When you were their only fighting chance?
The blood of this movement was shed for you
to soar
Pioneer new chapters for years to come
For trying times and eyes of hope
That will surely look to you

22min Abstract

Stand firm fall freely pass by never stop
momentum
We try too hard sometimes to strangle the
neck of control
I figured out of the maze
Feelings never led me astray
My ears perk up when my calling whispers to
enter the action
Rest my body in preparation for battle in case
it presents itself
Unwrap my being
Witness eternal light
I'm merely a lamp
Starter jacket concealed my inner shine when
I was 9
Controlled breaths made my shots more
accurate
Ocean breaths were too deep back then
Wells water whatever
Sink swim fly fire reborn
Babies I wish I knew
The little lies behind your lullaby is why I
can't sleep at night
Caps won't settle
Can't tuck in my vices

Get a grip
Slipped dimensions
Mention me with an address to address the
situation
Too much time wasted on ineffective
communication
What's your wavelength?
Silver tongue surfing drums
No sticks to protect the people from self
Seashore see more than wide eyes on wide
outs
Forfeit soul for dollars taxed robbery never
got a quarterback
Chances are your favorite star will fail you if
you live to see tomorrow
My concentration on inner conversations
ignites the constellations
Don't know why I'm this way I'm just grateful
for the path
Sweat waters the birds my seeds will see the
beach someday
Pen prophecies with a rhythm that can't be
fake
No replication
I've learned a lot

Enough to no you can't school me
Behind bars I've roamed free
Cellies called me yogi bear
Did they ever see or perceive the
contradiction in the duality
The truth can't hide from the Universe it was
born to speak to
What is evil? Everything around
Except what's inside
Accept this ride you too can Drexler glide
Possible when applied presence and proper
planning
No child left behind unless they were born
under the rainbow
I bend light to reach around the wardens of
right thinking
Unlock cells so brains believe in balance and
full capacity
No tree can take me to the places I dream of
between breaths
Take me to the source
Front porch prophet has been summoned
Someone needs to know my Angel number
My angle is aligned
Words escape me

Ford forgot to pick me up but it's fine
Rely on my own two feet to deliver me to the
hearts of men
Thought I knew it all till I lost it and went
searching for self
Stopped talking and arose by a ram in the
bush
I think he went to Suitland
I had to change clothes
Cheat code unlocked
Easy street came with a pass
It wasn't a social that made me a trust fund
baby
No lie
Let my hands fly forgetting the jaws of life
No accident
I ended up where I was supposed to be
Perfect plans promise profits personality
presenting poetry